Honu and Hina was painted with the help of many artists.
Mahalo to all of you who put your love into this book
and to those working to keep the harmony of nature intact.

Created by Naturally Hawaiian Publishing
1476 Ala Hekili Place
Honolulu, Hawai'i 96819

www.PatrickChingArt.com

Designed and Distributed by

ISLAND HERITAGE™
PUBLISHING
A DIVISION OF THE MADDEN CORPORATION
ISBN:1-61710-239-3
First Edition, Second Printing—2015

COP 150303

HONU and HINA

A Story of Coexistence

A Naturally Hawaiian Book
By Patrick Ching
and Friends

MESSAGE FROM THE AUTHOR

If you are a parent or teacher reading this book to children, or a child reading this book for yourself, you will soon notice that *Honu and Hina* is not a typical children's book.

This story is set in modern Hawai'i and presents facts about sea turtles and monk seals in Hawai'i, including references to real life and real dangers that these animals face.

Even though I have lived in Hawai'i all my life, I grew up never seeing a live sea turtle resting on the beach, or a monk seal that wasn't in a book. I was in my twenties when I finally met them close up by volunteering to study them in their protected habitat of the Northwestern Hawaiian Islands.

In recent years, *honu* (green sea turtle) and monk seals have been enjoying their protection and returning to beaches where they have not been seen for hundreds of years. Personally, I am thrilled to share the sand and sea with these animal friends.

The purpose of this book is to express in a story some history, culture, and conservation ideas about coexisting with animals and to look at the unique situations we face today.

In the back of the book you will find a pronunciation guide for words you may find difficult to say and more interesting facts about *honu* and monk seals.

I hope you enjoy reading *Honu and Hina* and that it will remind you to be kind to animals and each other. Most of all, think hard about the world you have been blessed with.

It is abundant with beauty and gifts.

What will you do in your life to *mālama*, take care of the *'āina*, the living earth?

Dedicated to Honey Girl, a gentle honu *that touched many lives,*

and Hina, a Hawaiian monk seal who inspired us to learn about nature.

Mahalo (Thank You) for showing us how to coexist (live well together).

The evening sky glowed with the light of a full moon as the waves crashed upon the sandy Hawaiian shore. High up on the beach, a patch of sand began to move. Honu, a baby green sea turtle, poked his tiny head out of the sand for his first look at the world above.

All of a sudden, dozens of baby sea turtles erupted from the sand like a volcano of little turtles, all pushing each other to make it to the top. The turtles scrambled down the beach, through the crashing waves, and out into the vast ocean.

As the full moon made room for the morning sun, another miracle of life was unveiled. A newborn monk seal pup saw her first sunrise. The shiny black pup had a round white birthmark on her hip that looked like the full moon.

As she grew, her black fur changed to silvery grey. The people of the island called her "Hina" after the goddess of the moon. Hina became quite famous because she was the first monk seal to be born on the island in recent history.

The years went by, and Honu and Hina grew older and stronger. Though they never met, they lived through many of the same adventures. They escaped dangers such as unattended fishing nets that could entangle them, hungry sharks that could bite them, and boats with propellers that could hit them.

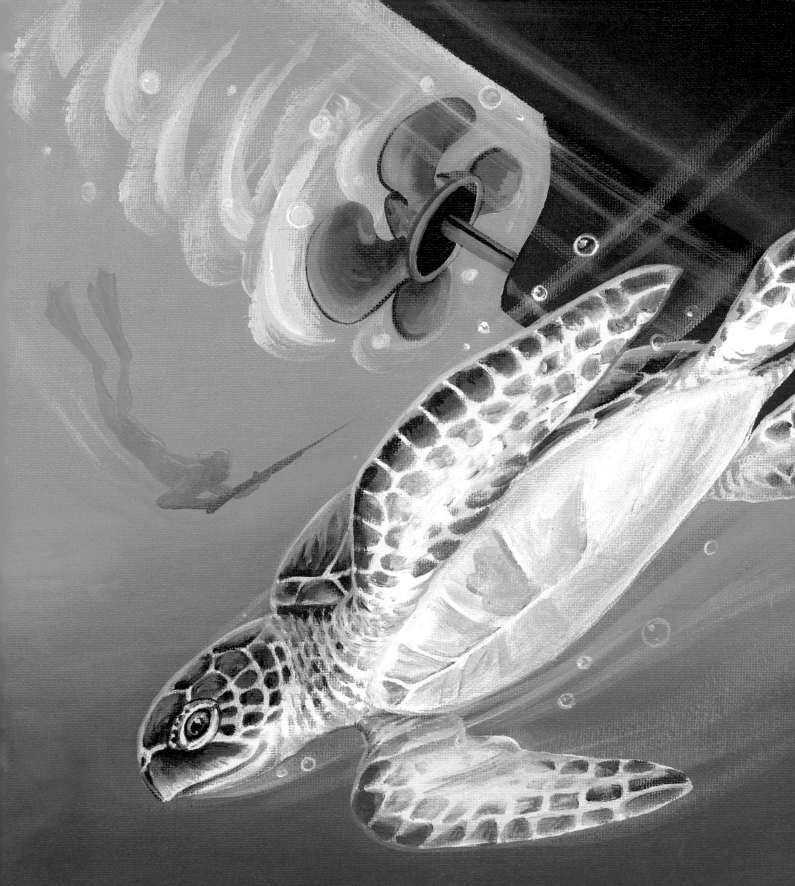

Many of their family members and ancestors were not so lucky. Some of them had been hunted by humans back in the days before laws protected turtles and seals. The laws were created because the numbers of these animals had dropped so low that they were in danger of becoming extinct.

One day, after Honu finished grazing on *limu* or "seaweed,"
he felt like going ashore to bask on the beach in the
midday sun. Honu came ashore and it was good.

He fell asleep at the water's edge as the lapping waves gently pushed his flippers back and forth.

Honu woke to a strange sound coming from a rock next to him. "Funny," he thought. "That rock wasn't there when I fell asleep." The rock started to breathe and snort, then it rolled over right onto Honu!

"Whoa!" said Honu. "You're not a rock?"

"No, I'm a monk seal," said Hina. "I thought YOU
were a rock, so I came to snuggle up next to you."

Honu and Hina became close friends and often came ashore to bask on the beach together. At many places, people would look after them by putting up rope barriers and reminding other people how important it was to give these animals enough space to rest undisturbed.

13

One day Honu and Hina swam to a beach where a man named Keoni and his daughter Pua were trying to catch fish. Keoni and Pua had seen turtles before, but this was the first time they had ever seen a seal at their favorite fishing spot.

It wasn't long before Hina began playing with a fish that was actually the bait on Keoni's fishing line. After Hina removed the bait fish from the hook, she and Honu swam away quickly. In the flurry, Honu brushed against the fishing line and its hook got stuck in his flipper.

"*Hana pa'a!* We hooked something!" screamed Pua as the fishing pole bent and the bell attached to it started ringing.

14

Keoni reeled the line in and saw that he had hooked Honu. "*Auwē*," (too bad) he said as he removed the hook and released Honu. Though he was hurt, Honu was thankful to be alive and free.

15

Keoni and Pua went home. They were excited to have seen a monk seal at the beach. They were also disturbed about the seal taking their bait and the *honu* getting hooked.

Pua told the story to her *Tūtū Kāne* (grandfather). *Tūtū Kāne* said, "I know *honu* well. In ancient times the *honu* was a respected food known for its life force. Only the *ali'i* (chiefs) were allowed to eat them. In my lifetime, we ate them at our family *lū'au* (feasts).

"Then the restaurants began to serve *honu*. As people's appetites for *honu* grew, the number of turtles declined. After a while *honu* became rare, and they would flee in fear at the sight of a human. That's when the modern day *kapu* (protective laws) began and *honu* started to come back. Some people would like to be able to eat *honu* again."

"How could anyone eat a turtle?" asked Pua.

Tūtū Kāne said, "The same way we eat *kalo* (taro), *iʻa* (fish), and *puaʻa* (pig). We respect our food and thank it for nourishing our bodies."

This gave Pua something to think about. "And what about the monk seal?" she asked.

Tūtū Kāne answered, "I have never seen one, but once in a while they were spotted in the ocean when I was a boy. Your aunty Kehau studies them at the university. She will know about monk seals."

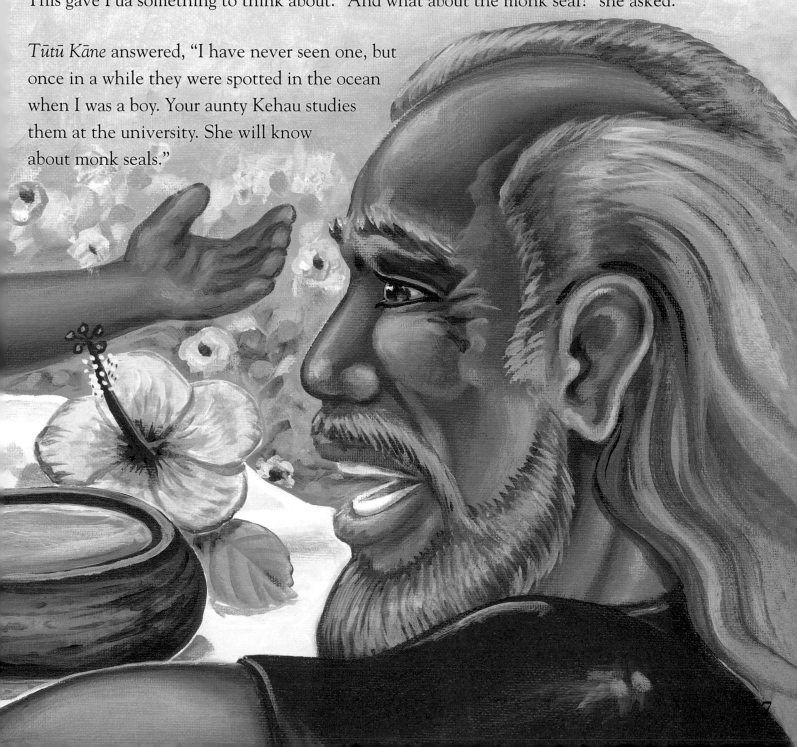

Aunty Kehau had researched the history of the Hawaiian monk seal. When Pua and her father came asking about the seals, Aunty Kehau gave them some answers.

The Hawaiian Monk Seal

"Monk seals have lived in the Hawaiian islands for millions of years. They are the oldest and rarest kind of seals in the world."

"The seals likely lived on all the Hawaiian Islands before there were people living in Hawai'i. After humans came to the islands, the seals lived mostly on the tiny remote Hawaiian islands called 'atolls.' These atolls lie to the northwest of the main islands. They are all that remain of large islands that once towered high above the sea."

"The Northwestern Hawaiian Islands are now called *Papahānaumokuākea*, named for the union of Earth Mother (*Papa*) and Sky Father (*Wākea*) that gave birth (*hānau*) to the islands (*moku*)."

Aunty Kehau showed Keoni and Pua some very old photographs of seals and *honu* on the tiny Hawaiian atolls.

Scientist George Willett with seal pup March 1913 Laysan Island, Hawaii
Photographed by Alfred M. Bailey

Pua was saddened by some of the pictures of the animals that were hunted by people. Aunty Kehau reminded her that it was now against the law to harm or kill these animals.

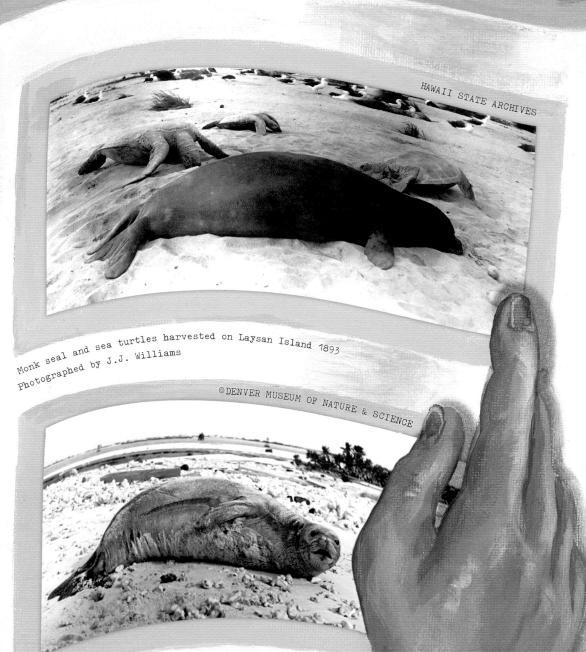

HAWAII STATE ARCHIVES

Monk seal and sea turtles harvested on Laysan Island 1893
Photographed by J.J. Williams

©DENVER MUSEUM OF NATURE & SCIENCE

Hawaii - Monk Seal Midway Atoll November 23, 1949
Photographed by Alfred M. Bailey

"In the 1980s, some of the monk seals began to swim down to the main Hawaiian islands to beaches where they had not lived for centuries. First Ni'ihau Island, then Kaua'i, then the rest. Soon seals were being born on all the main islands, sometimes even on crowded beaches!"

Aunty Kehau went on to say, "Just because you see more seals around the main islands nowadays, don't be fooled. They are a critically endangered species and need our help to survive."

Then Aunty Kehau told stories of other Hawaiian animals that had gone extinct, such as the ʻōʻō and the poʻouli birds. "'Extinct' means that they are gone and will never be seen alive on earth again," she said.

"The ʻalalā (Hawaiian crow), once plentiful and even considered a pest, is now completely gone in the wild. Just a small number of them live in a special building where scientists work to keep the species alive."

"There are happy stories of animal survival as well. Hawaii's state bird, the *nēnē* (goose), was once nearly extinct with only a couple dozen birds left in the wild. With people's help, the *nēnē* made a successful comeback and is now thriving for future generations to appreciate.

"*Koholā* (humpback whales) were also overhunted and are now protected and making a comeback. It is amazing to watch them "breaching" or jumping out of the water and splashing back into the sea.

"As for the Hawaiian monk seal, its numbers are so low that it could easily slip into extinction as the Caribbean monk seal did in the 1950s.

"Rather than getting mad at the monk seal for taking your bait or your favorite spot on the beach, consider its importance to the world and its natural right to exist," added Aunty Kehau.

On the way home, Keoni and Pua had a lot to discuss. They shared with *Tūtū Kāne* what they had learned.

The next day they all went to the beach to go fishing at their favorite place. There, on the very spot where they were going to set up, were Honu and Hina basking on the warm sand.

Keoni exclaimed, "Eh, they're in our spot!"

Tūtū Kāne put his hand on Keoni's shoulder. This was the first time he had ever seen a Hawaiian monk seal or even a live *honu* on the beach.

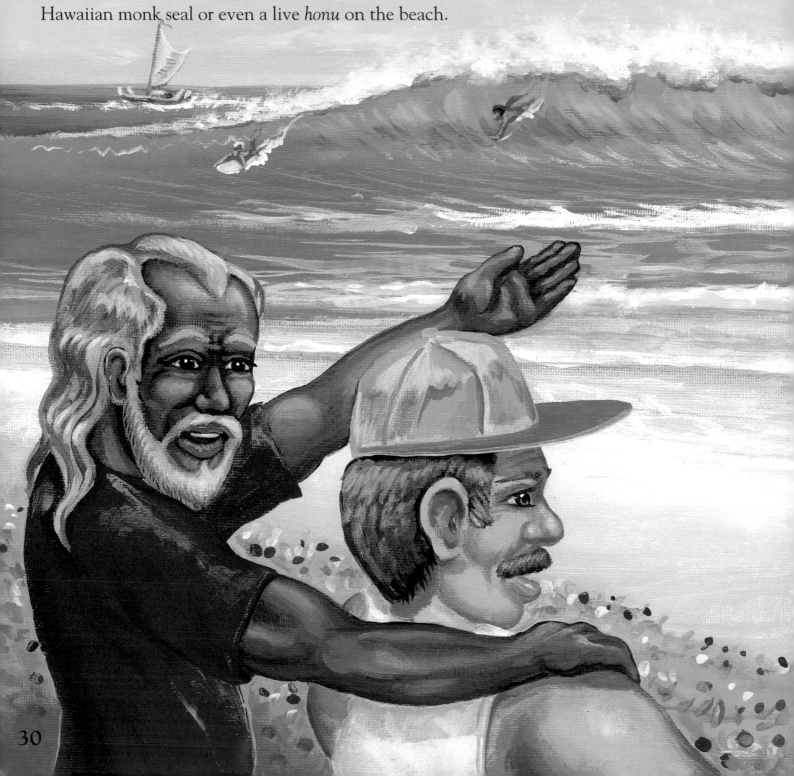

Tūtū Kāne spoke, and his son Keoni and granddaughter Pua listened closely to his words.

"I am thankful for the return of the *honu* and the monk seal. Look at them, how they share the beach. There is plenty of room for us all."

Keoni turned to his daughter Pua and said, "We can find a way to share the ʻāina, the living earth."

Pua smiled. She realized that she and her friends would soon be adults and that the fate of the ʻāina would be in the hands of their generation.

Honu and Hina rested peacefully on the beach.

Though their future seemed uncertain,
they knew that the present ...was a gift.

33

INTERESTING HONU FACTS

- There are five species of sea turtles found in Hawaiian waters. About 98% of all sea turtles in Hawai'i are the green sea turtles called *honu* in Hawaiian.
- A *honu* nest contains about a hundred eggs.
- *Honu* can live to be over a hundred years old.
- Adult male *honu* have very long tails and adult female *honu* have very short tails.
- The scales and outer layer of sea turtles' shells are made of keratin, the same kind of material that is in your fingernails and hair, and in fish scales and horse hooves.
- Hawaiian *honu* eat mostly algae or "seaweed" and sometimes jellyfish. It is important to keep plastic bags out of the ocean that a *honu* might mistake for a jellyfish meal.
- *Honu* go to certain areas of the reefs called "cleaning stations" where they are cleaned by fish that graze algae off of them.

INTERESTING MONK SEAL FACTS

- The Hawaiian name of the monk seal is *'īlio-holo-i-ka-uaua* which means "the dog that goes in the rough (seas)." Some people use shorter versions like *'īlio kai* or "sea dog."
- The monk seal gets its English name from its bald appearance, solitary habits, and a fold of skin behind its head that resembles a monk's hood.
- Adult monk seals weigh between 400 and 600 pounds.
- A mother monk seal usually gives birth to one pup each year. Baby monk seals are fed by their mother until they are about six weeks old. After that they must take care of themselves.
- In recent years, more seals are being born on the main Hawaiian Islands. At the same time, the overall number of monk seals is falling.
- Monk seals eat sea creatures like fish, eels, octopus, squid and lobster. They have been known to dive over 1,500 feet deep. That's a long way to go for a seafood dinner!

Patrick Ching

Pronunciation Guide

'āina (EYE-nah) - the living earth

'alalā (ah-lah-LAH) - Hawaiian crow

ali'i (ah-LEE-ee) - chief or royalty

atoll (AT-tole) - a coral island shaped like a ring

auwē (OW-way) - too bad!

Hana pa'a (HAH-nah PAH-ah)
     - make secure, as in set the hook

hānau (HAH-now) - to give birth

Hina (HEE-nah) - name of moon goddess

honu (HO-noo) - Hawaiian green sea turtle

i'a (EE-ah) - fish

'īlio-holo-i-ka-uaua (EE-lee-oh HO-lo ee kah-oo-a-oo-a)
     - dog that goes in the rough (seas)

'īlio kai (EE-lee-o kye) - sea dog, seal

kalo (KAH-lo) - taro

kapu (KAH-poo) - laws or restrictions

Kaua'i (kow-AH-ee) - name of island

Kehau (KAY-how) - name meaning dew drop

Keoni (kay-OH-nee)
     - Hawaiian pronunciation of the name John

koholā (ko-ho-LAH) - humpback whale

limu (LEE-moo) - algae or seaweed

lū'au (LOO-ow) - Hawaiian feast

mahalo (Mah-HAH-lo) - thank you

mālama (MAH-lah-mah) - take care of

moku (MOH-koo) - island

nēnē (nay-nay) - Hawaiian goose

Ni'ihau (NEE-ee-how) - name of island

'ō'ō (oh-oh) - Hawaiian honeyeater bird

Papa (PAH-pah) - Earth Mother

Papahānaumokuākea
     (pah-pah-HAH-now-mo-koo-ah-KAY-ah)
     - protected ocean area of the Northwestern
     Hawaiian Islands

po'ouli (po-oh-OO-lee) - honeycreeper bird

Pua (POO-ah) - name meaning flower

pua'a (poo-AH-ah) - pig

Tūtū Kāne (too-too KAH-nay) - grandfather

Wākea (WAH-kay-ah) - Sky Father

Patrick Ching